The Life Cycle of a

red fox

by Julian May
photographs by Allan Roberts
A CREATIVE EDUCATION MINI BOOK

Distributed Exclusively by
CHILDRENS PRESS, CHICAGO

Copyright © 1973 by Creative Educational Society, Inc. International copyrights reserved in all countries. No part of this book may be reproduced in any form, except for reviews, without permission in writing from the publisher. Printed in the United States.

ISBN: 0-87191-238-4
Library of Congress Catalog Card Number: 73-1224

Contents

6   On the prowl
12   The young
18   Finding food
24   Foxes and man
26   Different foxes
31   Range

the life cycle of a red fox

on the prowl

It is late winter and a red fox prowls about in search of food. Its slender body wears a coat of beautiful, warm fur. The fox does not mind the winter cold. But food is not so easy to find in cold weather. The fox must search far and wide for small animals to eat. Most red foxes live in wild places, but sometimes they come into towns and cities.

People hardly ever see the fox, because it hunts mostly at night and at twilight. When it moves about, it hides among bushes or other plants. It knows that human beings are a danger to it, so it hides when people are near.

The fox is a member of the dog family. Its body is about two feet long. A large, bushy tail measures about 15 inches more. The fox has a pointed snout and large ears.

The red fox lives by its wits. Like most dogs, it is an intelligent animal—a hunter that must outwit both its prey and its enemies if it is to survive.

Its senses of smell, sight, and hearing are very sharp. Its whiskers help it feel its way in the dark. The rather long legs of the fox enable it to dash about quickly. The fluffy tail is a warm muff in winter.

Male and female red foxes look almost exactly alike. In the eastern part of North America, the fox is often reddish gold with dark ears and legs. Farther west, one may find "red" foxes that are almost black. The silver fox is a red fox with a silvery-gray coat. All true red foxes have white underparts and a white tip to the tail. Other foxes do not have a white tail-tip.

the young

In winter, the male and female fox live together as mates. They will stay with each other to raise the young. Late in winter, they make a den. Sometimes it is an old hole made by some other animal. Or the foxes may dig their own hole in soft earth. The den has soft grass inside. Only the mother uses it, while the father sleeps outside.

About 51 days after mating, the pups are born.

From four to nine young foxes are born in each litter. The birth month is usually March or April. At first, the babies have their eyes closed. Their fur is brownish and fluffy. The mother does not leave her pups for the first few days. She feeds them with milk from her body and grooms them with her tongue. The babies spend most of their time eating and sleeping.

After two or three days, the mother begins hunting for food again. Her mate often brings meat for her to share. The babies grow quickly and their eyes open.

After about five weeks, the pups are strong enough to come out of the den. Their eyes are blue—but later they will turn brown. The pups begin to grow their adult coats of fur.

Baby foxes are very playful. They wrestle with each other and pounce on each other. They seem to fight a lot without getting hurt. This is really practice for the time when they will have to hunt in order to live.

Both parents guard the young. If an enemy comes near, the pups dash back into the den. An adult fox leads the enemy away from the den and gets him lost.

In former days, foxes might be attacked by golden eagles and wolves. Both of these predators are getting rare, and so are the bobcats and lynxes that also hunt foxes.

Among the main enemies of the fox these days are coyotes, domestic dogs, and man. But the fox is so crafty that it is not often caught. It is a very abundant animal and shows no sign of disappearing from the earth.

finding food

At first, the parents help the babies find food. But soon the pups are finding mice and small rabbits by themselves. They learn to spring quickly at their prey. Their tails help them to keep their balance as they twist and turn.

The young fox in the picture shows his wooly undercoat. Soon he will grow his red, rainproof outer coat.

Soon after the young foxes come out of the den, the parents begin giving them meat to eat. The pups also feed on their mother's milk.

By the time they are nine weeks old, they are ready to eat the same food their parents do. They begin by catching grasshoppers and other insects. Their teeth grow, and slowly they become better hunters.

In summer, the foxes will feed on fruits as well as meat. They love wild berries. They also eat birds and their eggs, and larger dead animals that they may find. Uneaten food is hidden away until it is needed.

Red foxes can swim well, and they will catch and eat frogs, muskrats, and turtles. Parents continue to feed their young until fall.

For about five months, the parents work together to teach their young how to make a living as hunters. They also teach the pups how to avoid traps, and how to confuse an enemy by circling around him or by walking in water to destroy their scent.

In fall, the young foxes are ready to go off by themselves. They hunt all winter, hiding in dens when it is very cold.

foxes and man

For many years, people did not understand how wild hunters such as the fox could be helpful to man. People saw foxes stealing chickens and thought they were worthless pests. Rewards were set up for killing them. They were not only hunted, but also trapped and poisoned.

Many foxes were killed, but still more escaped. And now we know that foxes are necessary and very useful.

Today, laws help protect foxes from reckless killing by man. We know that foxes hunt rats, mice, ground squirrels, and rabbits. Without foxes, the plant-eaters can multiply so quickly that they do great harm to crops.

Wild foxes are still trapped for their beautiful fur. But more and more fox fur now comes from animals raised on fur ranches. In this way, people can wear fur coats without upsetting the balance of nature.

different foxes

Several close relatives of the red fox live in North America. The gray fox, which lacks a white tip to its tail, is found in many of the same places where the red fox lives. But the gray fox is not so bold as the red. It prefers thick woods or swamps. Gray foxes have blackish gray coats, sometimes mixed with red or yellow. They are more common in warmer climates than the red foxes.

The smallest foxes in North America live on the dry plains and deserts of the West. The swift fox of the Great Plains is about the size of a house cat, with yellowish fur and a black tip to its tail. Its close relative, the kit fox, is even smaller and more slender. Its coat is pale gray. Both foxes have very large ears that help them listen for their prey. They feed on mice, rats, and insects. They are helpful to man and sometimes come to stare at people.

The arctic fox lives in the far North. It is found in Alaska, Canada, northern Europe, and northern Asia. Its ears are tiny so that they will not be easily frozen. It also has heavy fur on its feet.

During the summer, the arctic fox has a brownish or blue-gray coat. In winter, some arctic foxes turn pure white while others are blue. When food is scarce, the fox comes south into warmer lands. It feeds mostly on rodents.

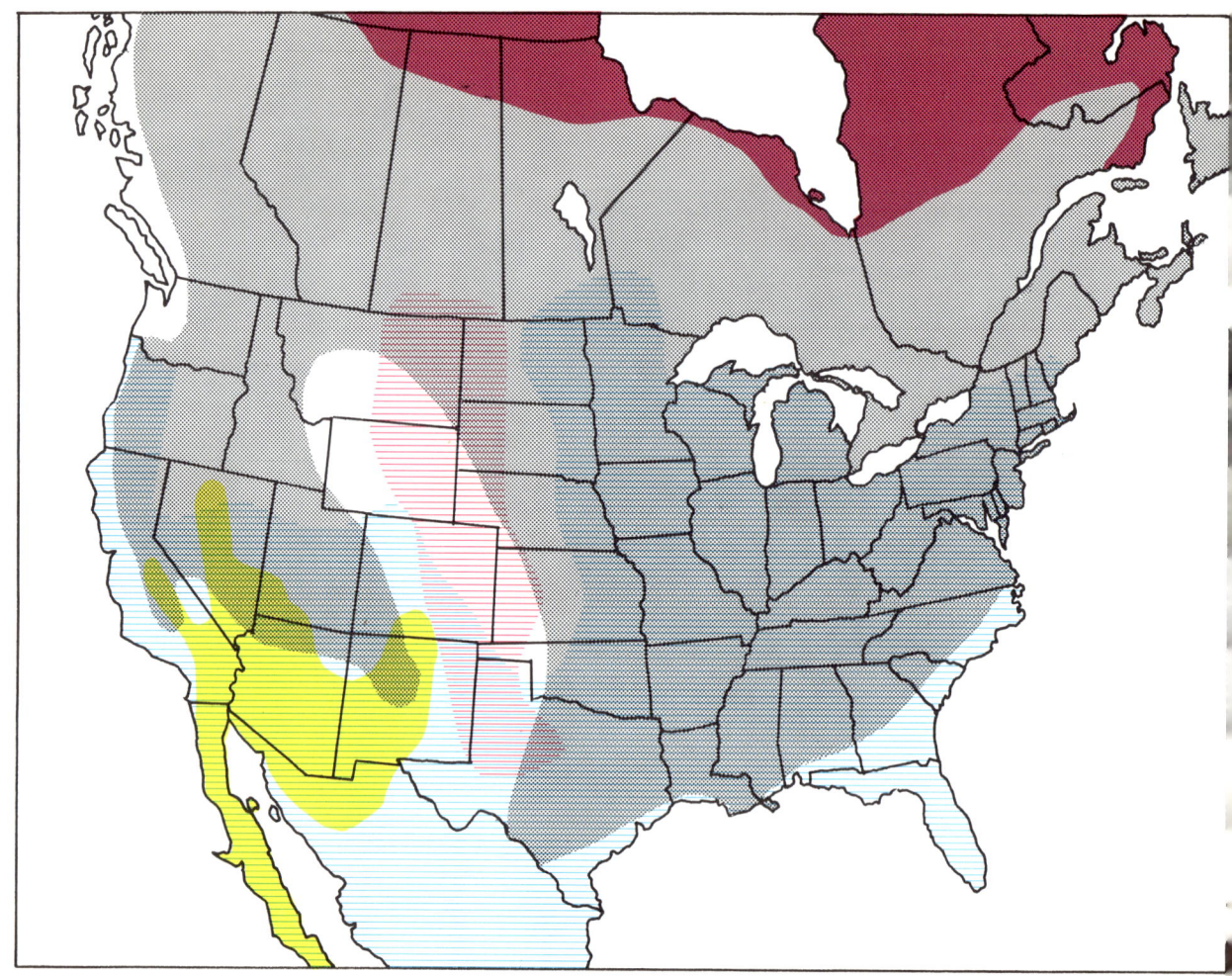

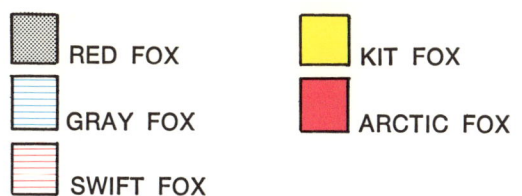

range

The red fox lives in most parts of the United States and Canada. It is not found in the central Great Plains, in Florida, or in the desert Southwest. Gray foxes are most common in warmer lands and range southward into Mexico and South America. Kit and swift foxes are becoming rare because they eat poisoned bait intended for coyotes. Now they only live in remote western deserts.

Other Creative Mini Books

Life Cycles

Life Cycle of a Bullfrog
Life Cycle of a Raccoon
Life Cycle of an Opossum
Life Cycle of a Moth
Life Cycle of a Rabbit
Life Cycle of a Fox
Life Cycle of a Turtle
Life Cycle of a Butterfly

World We Know

Fishes We Know
Birds We Know
Reptiles We Know
Mammals We Know
Insects We Know